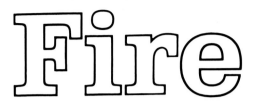

Fire

Andrew Charman

Watts Books
London • New York • Sydney

© 1993 Watts Books

Watts Books
96 Leonard Street
London EC2A 4RH

Franklin Watts Australia
14 Mars Road
Lane Cove
NSW 2066

UK ISBN: 0 7496 1145 6

10 9 8 7 6 5 4 3 2 1

Series editor: Pippa Pollard
Editor: Claire Llewellyn
Design: Shaun Barlow
Cover design: Edward Kinsey
Artwork: Ian Thompson
Cover artwork: Hugh Dixon
Picture research: Ambreen Husain

Educational advisor: Joy Richardson

A CIP catalogue record for this book
is available from the British Library

Printed in Italy by G. Canale & C. SpA

Contents

Fire for life

Planet Earth is only fit for life because it is warmed by the Sun. The Sun is a huge fiery ball. Without its heat, the earth would be too cold for us to survive.

On Earth we use fire for many things. We use it to make things and to cook. Fire also gives us energy for heating our homes and for **transport.**

▽ Very hot objects produce light. This is why the Sun is so bright. You can damage your eyes by looking directly at the Sun without sunglasses.

Fire in the earth

Deep down in the centre, or core, of the earth it is very hot – about 4,500° **Centigrade**. The rocks of the outer core are not so deep, but they are still so hot that they are liquid, or **molten**. Above this is the mantle. Water which is heated deep in the earth sometimes shoots to the surface in spouts, called geysers.

▷ A geyser is a spout of boiling hot water. The water is heated deep in the earth.

▽ Imagine you could take a sample of the earth from the crust to the core. You would be able to see the different layers. The deeper you go into the earth, the hotter it gets.

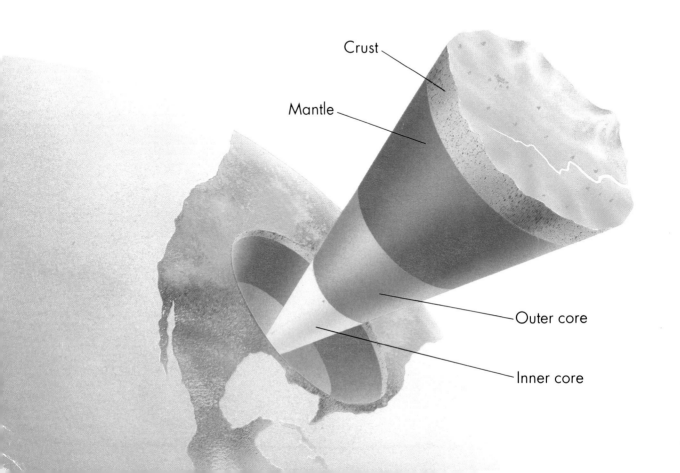

Crust

Mantle

Outer core

Inner core

◁These monkeys are Japanese macaques. They are keeping warm by bathing in a hot spring.

Volcanoes

The molten rock deep down in the earth is called **magma**. Volcanoes are openings in the hard surface, or **crust**, of the earth, through which magma and gases sometimes escape. This is called an eruption. When magma reaches the surface of the earth, it is called **lava.** When lava cools, it hardens into rock.

▽ An erupting volcano will hurl lava, smoke and pieces of rock high into the air. It may destroy nearby towns and villages.

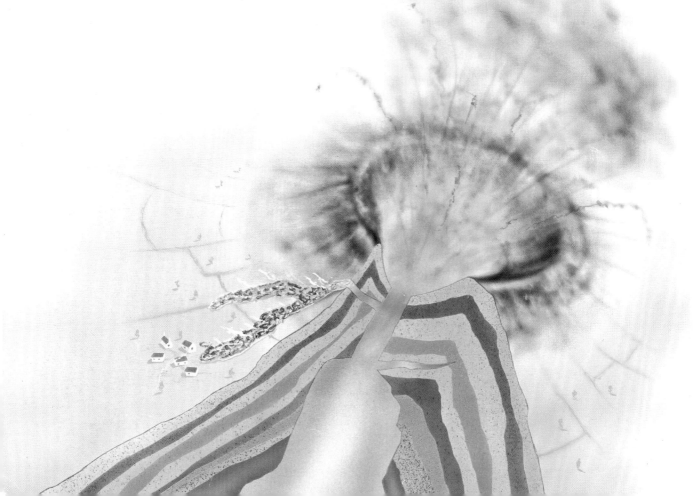

◁ This hill is really the inside of an old volcano. It is made of solid lava.

▽ When a volcano erupts the red-hot lava travels fast. It burns everything in its path.

7

What is fire?

Fire is the heat and light we feel and see when something burns. Fires often have flames. They usually need the **gas** called **oxygen** in order to burn. Air contains oxygen. This is why fanning or blowing onto a fire makes it burn faster. Most things will burn. Some burn at a lower **temperature** than others.

▷ Many farmers burn off the stubble in their fields. They need to be careful. Fire spreads easily out in the open. This is because air contains oxygen.

▽ Oil is being burnt at the top of this rig. It is a fuel that burns easily.

▷ Paper catches fire easily, but soon burns itself out.

9

Making fire

Long ago, people discovered ways to make fire. Rubbing two materials together makes them heat up. If they heat up enough, some of them will catch fire. Also, striking a stone or a piece of metal with another hard material will sometimes make a spark. A spark may start a fire if it falls onto something which burns easily, like dried grass.

▽ This blacksmith is wearing goggles to protect his eyes from the sparks that fly up as he grinds an iron bar.

▷ This person is starting a fire with a fire-drill. He is rubbing two pieces of wood together.

◁ The metal wheels of a train will sometimes make sparks fly as they run along the metal rails.

▷ Striking one hard object against another can make a spark. This is another way to start a fire.

Fire for warmth and light

In many parts of the world, people burn open fires to keep warm. They put wood or coal on the fire to keep it burning. Modern heating systems burn gas or oil. The flame is used to heat water.

Light is given off by very hot objects such as a burning candle or a hot wire inside a bulb.

▽ Wood burns well and is easily found. Open fires that burn wood keep people warm in many parts of the world.

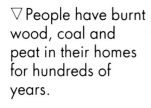

▽ People have burnt wood, coal and peat in their homes for hundreds of years.

◁▷ Simple lighting, such as a candle, uses a flame. The thin wire inside some bulbs glows when it is hot. It gives off a brighter light.

Fire for cooking

Long ago, people found out how to cook food with fire. Food can be cooked outside over an open flame. A lot of heat is lost in the open air. Simple stoves burn wood without losing so much heat. Modern gas cookers use a flame which you can control. Electric cookers have a metal ring which gets very hot.

▷ Wood-burning stoves use less fuel. They save wood as well as the time it takes people to collect it.

▽ You can cook food over a simple fire. You need to protect the food from the flames or it will burn before it cooks.

▷ Modern cookers are easy to control. They waste very little heat.

Fire in industry

Fire is used in **industry** to change materials. It can change a metal by making it easier to bend. Fire can also melt a metal into a liquid. The metal can then be moulded into a new shape. Bricks are blocks of wet clay that have been 'cooked'. The heat dries them out and makes them hard. Plates and cups are made in the same way.

▷ In a hot enough furnace, metal will melt into a liquid.

▷ Pots, plates and bricks made of clay can all be heated in a kiln to make them hard.

▷ The materials for making glass are first heated. The glass can then be shaped. This man is hand-blowing a piece of glass.

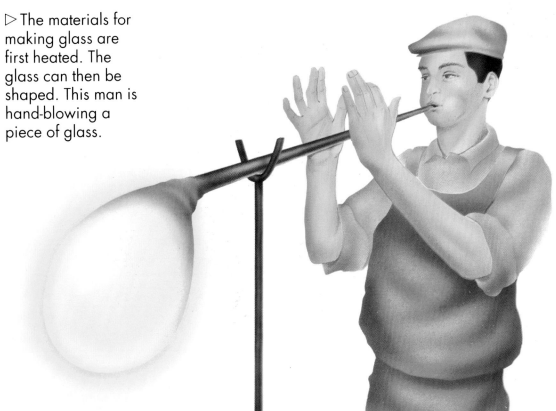

Energy from fire

Coal, gas, oil and wood are all kinds of **fuel.** We burn fuels to release energy. This energy can then be used in many ways. Cars, trucks, planes, trains and ships all burn fuel to make them move. We also burn fuel in some power stations. This makes heat, which boils water to make steam. The steam drives machinery which makes **electricity.**

▷ Jet engines burn large amounts of fuel. This gives the plane the energy to take off.

▽ Most vehicles burn petrol in their engines. Petrol is made from oil.

▽ Trains can be driven by steam. The energy comes from the coalfire in the engine.

▷ Many power
stations burn coal to
make electricity.

Forest fires

Every summer, huge areas of forest are destroyed by fire. Most of the fires are started by people who camp and cook in the forest. The grass and wood is very dry. The smallest spark may make it burn. Forest fires can also be started by lightning. A flash of lightning is a huge spark of electricity. If it strikes a tree, it will catch fire.

▷ Every year there are huge forest fires. They destroy thousands of plants and animals.

▽ Visitors to the forest need to take great care. A smouldering fire may set grass and brushwood alight.

◁ A forest will grow back after a fire, but this will take many years.

Pollution by fire

Burning fuels give off smoke and gases. Some of these can be dangerous. When there is too much of these gases in the air, it becomes **polluted**. Plants and animals suffer in polluted air. We can help to stop pollution by burning fewer fuels. People are finding new ways to get energy from the Sun and the wind.

▷ All fires give off gases. Burning rubber gives off dangerous black smoke.

▽ Forests help to clean the air. Many of them are being burnt down to make room for cattle. We should save them.

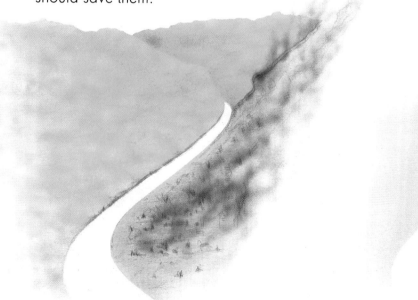

22

▽ This solar furnace
gathers energy from
the Sun without
causing pollution.

Disasters with fire

Terrible disasters can be caused by fire. When volcanoes erupt they release red hot lava. The lava burns as it flows downhill. Planes and cars sometimes catch fire when they crash. The fire is often made worse because of the fuel the vehicle is carrying. Buildings often catch fire because of accidents with heaters, cookers or cigarettes.

▷ A fire will spread if the building contains furniture and fittings that burn easily.

▽ Planes carry huge amounts of fuel. In the case of an accident, this can cause very serious fires.

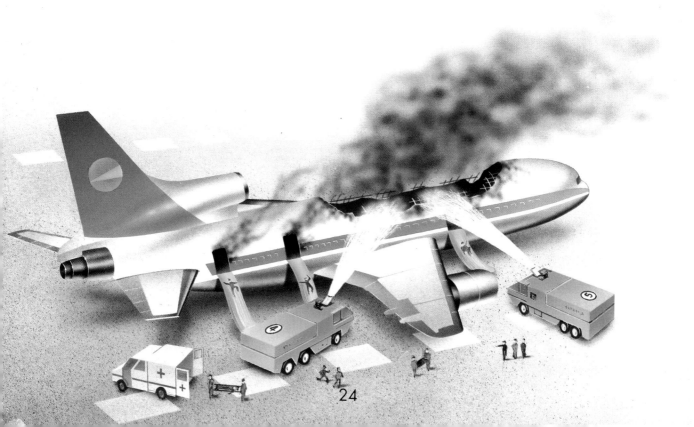

Fire fighting

Fire fighting is a highly skilled and dangerous job. People who fight fires are trained to know which part of the fire to attack first. They also know how to rescue people and prevent the fire from spreading. There are different kinds of equipment for different fires. Forest fires are sometimes put out by water sprayed from planes.

▷ Small aircraft are used to fight fires that spread over a large area.

▷ Every home should have a fire extinguisher for putting out small fires.

▷ Fire fighters carry hoses and other equipment on their fire engines. They connect the hoses to water pipes below the street.

Fire and safety

Fires can injure and kill people. They also destroy buildings, animals and plants. It is important to know how to prevent a fire. You also need to know what to do if a fire does start. Fire spreads when there is plenty of air. Closing doors and windows, or covering a small fire with a blanket, will help to stop it spreading.

▷A fire drill is a good way for people to practise what to do if ever there is a fire.

▽ Pressing the button on a fire alarm will set off a bell. This warns other people that a fire has started.

△ Every home should have a smoke alarm. This gives a very early warning of a fire.

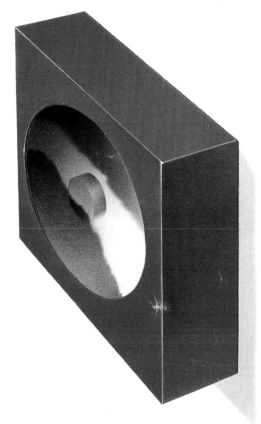

▽ Most new furniture is made from materials which do not burn easily.

▷ The fire exits in public buildings are always clearly marked.

Things to do

- Make a small collection of things which have been made or changed by heat. These could be glass, a moulded metal, pottery, cooked food and so on.

- Make a fire code for your home. Write down where the fire exits are. Think of a way to warn other people of a fire. Make sure you have a smoke detector and a fire extinguisher.

- Make a collage on the theme of fire. You could included pictures of the Sun, volcanoes, forest fires and fire fighting.

- See if you can visit a glass foundry where people are blowing glasses or bottles from molten glass.

Glossary

Centigrade A scale used to measure how hot or cold something is. Water freezes at 0°C and boils at 100°C.

Crust The hard outer surface which covers the earth.

Electricity The flow of an electric current. Its energy is used to make light and heat, and to power a motor.

Energy The ability to do work. When an object moves, it has energy. Heat and light are also forms of energy.

Fuel A material like wood or coal which releases energy when it is burnt.

Furnace A place which can contain a fire. Furnaces are used to heat or melt things.

Gas A substance that is not a solid or liquid. Air is a mixture of gases.

Industry Work which is done in factories to make goods.

Lava Molten rock that flows from a volcano.

Magma Molten rock inside the earth.

Molten Metal or rock which is turned to liquid by very great heat.

Oxygen A gas which nearly all living things need to survive.

Polluted Spoilt by harmful substances.

Temperature How hot or cold something is.

Transport Vehicles to move people or objects from one place to another.

Index